Crock Pot Cookbook for Busy People

Simple And Fast Recipes To Enjoy Food Every Day. Discover Amazing Recipes To Lose Weight And Lower Risk Of Heart Disease

Clara Smith

Table of Contents

Introduction

The crockpot has long been a favorite kitchen implement for the 'set-it-and-forget-it' meal. It's a wonderful invention by whoever thought it up, and it has saved many a few dollars on electricity by not needing to keep the stove and oven on for extended hours and all day. So, what really is a crockpot?

A crockpot is also called a slow cooker or a casserole crockpot. These nicknames refer to the same kitchen appliance, and it is one of the most used reheating methods today. It is basically a cooker with a glazed ceramic bowl that has a tight sealing lid. It is because of the liquid that will go in with the food. The crockpot is then plugged into an electrical socket in the kitchen for it to work.

The crockpot slow cooking method involves basically depositing the ingredients you desire to cook into the crockpot bowl (usually by stirring it with a wooden spoon or a ladle), adding the liquid of choice, cooking it for a few hours until it's done. These used to be the standard cooking methods in kitchens, and they have stayed the same with the invention of the crockpot. Nowadays, most crockpots have interiors thermostatically controlled to ensure that it's set at the right temperature during the cooking process to not over-cook your meals.

The best in crockpot slow cooking is finding that low and slow recipe. Recipes that are low in time length are usually very low in steps, and not much work is involved. It usually leads to the much sought after 'set it and forget it' kind of meal. Imagine not having to watch your meals cook slowly as you work on other tasks; you can avoid the temptation of peeking or checking on it too often and not having to worry about burning or crusting on the sides of your crockpot. When cooking at low heat, you don't have to worry about your meal exploding all over the kitchen or all the grease falling out and sticking to the bottom of your crock.

The best use of crockpot slow cooking is the convenience of the food, especially during holidays and parties. You can set the crockpot down on the table, and everyone can serve themselves. It is an excellent and great way to spend time with your guests and treat them well. There is nothing cheesier than eating the same dish fondue style. You get to enjoy slow cooking hotdogs for hours and hours without little ones surreptitiously taking off the top and poaching them in the pool of oil sitting beside the dish.

A crockpot is a very good way to use leftovers for a delicious meal. If you cook a large meal regularly and you have leftovers, put them in a crockpot with a liquid and let it cook. It will double the amount of food leftover or fed to the cat at the end of the week.

Crockpot cooking generally saves time, but it is also a low-budget way to cook. Slow cooking food can save you money because they are usually very low and easy to make. In fact, it is even possible to cook a meal with the last few pennies in your wallet. If you're on a tight budget and you don't have much to spend on your meals, the crockpot is the way to go.

Crockpots even make for a great gift since it's made in many shapes and sizes, from the really small, 1-quart crockpot to the huge 8 quarts or more. Any shape or size would be a welcome gift for anyone because everyone eats. Any occasion could be a good time to give someone a crockpot, and the more occasions you can name, the more crockpots you could make as gifts.

CHAPTER 1:

Breakfast

1. Keto English Muffin

Preparation time: 15 minutes

Cooking time: 2 hours

Servings: 6

Ingredients:

- 3 tbsp almond flour
- ½ tbsp coconut flour
- 1 tbsp butter (or coconut oil)
- 1 egg
- 1 pinch sea salt

- ½ tsp baking soda
- salt (as desired)

Directions:

1. Take a medium-sized skillet, melt the butter. It takes usually 20-30 seconds. Pour coconut and almond flour, egg, salt into the melted butter and stir everything well.
2. Take the skillet from the heat and add baking soda. Open the Crock Pot, spray the bottom of the Crock Pot with cooking spray. Pour the mixture.
3. Cover the lid and put on low for 2 hours. Check the readiness with a fork. Remove the baked muffin from the Crock Pot and eat with bacon slices, cheese or other breakfast staples. Bon Appetite!

Nutrition:

Calories: 222

Carbs: 5g

Fat: 19g Protein: 8g

2. Cauliflower Casserole with Tomato and Goat Cheese

Preparation time: 15 minutes

Cooking time: 3 hours & 1 minutes

Servings: 12

Ingredients:

- 6 cups cauliflower florets
- 4 tsp olive oil
- 1 tsp dried oregano
- ½ tsp salt
- ½ tsp ground pepper
- 2 oz. goat cheese crumbled

The Sauce:

- 1 tsp olive oil
- 3 cloves garlic

- 1 can crushed tomatoes (28 oz.)
- 2 bay leaves
- ¼ tsp salt
- ¼ cup minced flat-leaf parsley

Directions:

1. Wash the cauliflower, remove the leaves and core, cut it into small pieces (florets). Spray the bottom of the Crock Pot with cooking spray, put the cauliflower florets on the bottom of it, add olive oil, oregano, and pepper. Salt if desired.
2. Cover and cook on low for 2 hours until the cauliflower florets get tender and a little bit brown color.
3. While the cauliflower is cooking prepare the sauce: peel the garlic cloves and mince it. Take a medium-sized skillet, heat the olive oil, add garlic and cook 1 minute, stir it thoroughly all the time.

4. Add the crushed tomatoes and bay leaves, let it simmer for some minutes. Remove the bay leaves, dress with pepper and salt. You may also add parsley if you want.

5. Pour the sauce over the cauliflower florets in the Crock Pot once the time is over. Spread the Goat cheese over the dish, cover the Crock Pot and continue cooking for 1 hour on low until the cheese is melted. Serve warm!

Nutrition:

Calories: 170

Carbs: 10g

Fat: 13g

Protein: 7g

3. Turkish Breakfast Eggs

Preparation time: 15 minutes

Cooking time: 4 hours

Servings: 9

Ingredients:

- 1 tbsp olive oil
- 2 onions
- 1 red pepper
- 1 red chili, small
- 8 cherry tomatoes
- 1 slice keto bread
- 4 eggs
- 2 tbsp milk
- small bunch of parsley
- 4 tbsp natural yogurt at will

- pepper at will

Directions:

1. Peel the onions and chop finely. Wash parsley and chop finely. Wash the cherry tomatoes and dry with a paper towel.

2. Wash the pepper and chili, take off the seeds from the bell pepper and slice. Cube the keto bread. Spray the inside of the Crock Pot with oil or cooking spray.

3. In a large skillet, heat the oil, add the onions, pepper, and chili. Stir everything together. Cook until the veggies begin to soften.

4. Put them in the Crock Pot and add the cherry tomatoes and bread, stir everything well. Cover and cook on low for 4 hours. Season with fresh parsley and yogurt. Bon Appetite!

Nutrition:

Calories: 353

Carbs: 32g

Fat: 16g

Protein: 20g

4. Pumpkin Spice Pie

Preparation time: 15 minutes

Cooking time: 3 hours

Servings: 4

Ingredients:

- 1 ½ cup raw pecans
- ¾ cup Swerve Sweetener
- 1/3 cup coconut flour
- ¼ cup unflavored whey protein powder
- 2 tsp baking powder
- 1 ½ tsp ground cinnamon
- 1 tsp ground ginger
- ¼ tsp ground cloves
- ¼ tsp salt
- 1 cup pumpkin puree

- 4 large eggs
- ¼ cup butter melted
- 1 tsp vanilla extract

Directions:

1. Spread the bottom of the Crock Pot with cooking spray. Grind the pecans in the food processor until the coarse meal, but don't let turn them into the butter.
2. Transfer pecans to the bowl and whisk together, add coconut flour, sweetener, baking powder, whey protein powder, ginger, cinnamon, salt garlic and whisk once more.
3. Mix in another bowl pumpkin puree, cracked eggs, vanilla, butter until well mixed. Join everything together, add this mixture to the Crock Pot and set on low for 3 hours.
4. As soon as the top of the pie is barely firm to the touch the pumpkin spice pie is ready. Bon Appetite!

Nutrition: Calories: 150 Carbs: 15g Fat: 9g Protein: 1g

5. Broccoli Omelet

Preparation time: 15 minutes

Cooking time: 2 hours

Servings: 14

Ingredients:

- 6 large Eggs
- ½ cup fat milk
- ¼ tsp Salt
- ½ tsp Pepper
- ¼ tsp garlic powder
- ¼ tsp chili powder
- shortening or non-stick cooking spray (for greasing the crockpot)
- 1 yellow onion, small
- 3 cloves garlic

- 1 cup fresh broccoli florets
- 1 tbsp parmesan cheese
- 1-2 cups cheddar cheese
- 1 tomato chopped, medium
- ¼ cup green onions

Directions:

1. Peel the yellow onion and cut it. Peel the garlic and press, shred the cheese and wash the medium red tomato, dry with paper towel and cut also. Chop the green onions.
2. Take a cooking spray and spread it over the bottom and all the sides of your Crock Pot, just to prevent sticking.
3. Crack the eggs into a large bowl, add the cup of milk mix well, add all the species and mix it once more carefully.
4. Add the onions to the mixture, then garlic, Parmesan cheese, and broccoli florets. Continue whisking it thoroughly.

5. Put your mixture into the Crock Pot, cover and cook on high for 2 hours. As soon as the time is over, with using the long keen knife cut along the edge of the Crock Pot into quarters.
6. Take your omelet to the plate and serve with remaining cheddar and green chopped onions. Bon Appetite!

Nutrition:

Calories: 410

Carbs: 7g

Fat: 31g

Protein: 31g

CHAPTER 2:

Mains

6. Pulled Pork Sliders

Preparation time: 15 minutes

Cooking time: 8 hours

Servings: 8

Ingredients:

- 1 medium onion, chopped
- ½ cup ketchup
- 1/3 cup cider vinegar
- ¼ cup tomato paste
- 2 tablespoons sweet paprika

- 3 teaspoons sea salt
- 2 tablespoons Worcestershire sauce
- 1 ¼ teaspoon black pepper
- 2 1/2 lbs. pork butt, cut into 2 pieces
- 12 slider buns

Directions:

1. Combine all your ingredients in your Crock Pot, except the pork and buns. Mix these ingredients together using a spoon. Add the 2 pieces of pork butt into the Crock Pot. Cover and cook on low for 8 hours.
2. After the 8 hours cook time remove the pork and shred it in a bowl with a fork, along with remaining sauce. Toast the slider buns and add some pulled pork onto the buns. Top with pickles and serve.

Nutrition:Calories: 320 Fat: 8.5 g Carbs: 25.7 g Protein: 35 g

7. Chicken Fajitas

Preparation time: 15 minutes

Cooking time: 4 hours

Servings: 9

Ingredients:

- 2 lbs. chicken breasts halves, boneless, skinless
- 1 (14.5-ounce) can of tomatoes, petite diced with green chilies
- 1 large yellow onion, halved, sliced
- 4 garlic cloves, minced
- 1 red, orange, and green bell pepper, julienned
- 2 ½ teaspoons chili powder
- 2 teaspoons ground cumin
- 1 teaspoon paprika
- ¾ teaspoon pepper
- 2 tablespoons fresh lime juice

- 1 tablespoon honey

For Serving:

- Flour tortillas, cilantro, salsa, sour cream, guacamole, Monterrey jack or cheddar cheese.

Directions:

1. Pour half of the can of tomatoes in the bottom of your Crock Pot. Top with half of the peppers and half of onions. Sprinkle in garlic and top with chicken breasts.
2. In a mixing bowl whisk together cumin, chili powder, coriander, salt and pepper. Evenly sprinkle half of the seasoning over chicken breasts then flip chicken and sprinkle in the remainder.
3. Top with remaining tomatoes, then layer with remaining peppers and onions. Cover and cook on HIGH for 4 hours, or until the chicken has cooked through and veggies are tender. Remove chicken and cut into strips.
4. In a small bowl whisk honey and lime juice together. Remove about a cup of broth from pot and discard. Add honey mix into

crock pot, along with chicken strips and season with additional salt.

5. Gently toss. Serve on warmed tortillas with sour cream and salsa, guacamole and cheese.

Nutrition:

Calories: 224

Fat: 7.8 g

Carbs: 7.5 g

Protein: 30.1 g

8. Balsamic Chicken

Preparation time: 15 minutes

Cooking time: 3 hours

Servings: 4

Ingredients:

- 10 chicken thighs, boneless, skinless
- 1 (16-ounce) package frozen white pearl onions
- 2 tablespoons extra virgin olive oil
- 8 ounces white button mushrooms, quartered
- 5 garlic cloves, minced
- 2 stems rosemary, fresh
- 1 bay leaf
- ¾ cup balsamic vinegar
- 1 cup chicken stock
- 3 tablespoons tomato paste

- ¼ cup brown sugar
- sea salt and black pepper to taste
- 1 tablespoon butter
- ½ cup pomegranate seeds
- ¼ cup fresh parsley, chopped

Directions:

1. Season chicken thighs with sea salt and black pepper. Heat the olive oil in large pan over medium-high heat and brown the thighs in batches for about 5 minutes on each side.
2. Remove thighs from pan and set aside. Layer the pearl onions, button mushrooms, rosemary, garlic and bay leaf in Crock Pot. Add in the browned chicken thighs.
3. Mix balsamic vinegar, chicken stock, tomato paste, and brown sugar in mixing bowl. Season with salt and pepper. Pour mixture over chicken and cover and cook on HIGH for 3 hours.

Nutrition: Calories: 280 Fat: 10.5 g Carbs: 13.8 g Protein: 31.2 g

9. Sweet & Sour Chicken

Preparation time: 15 minutes

Cooking time: 3 hours

Servings: 8

Ingredients:

For Chicken:

- 2 lbs. chicken breasts, boneless, skinless, cut into chunks
- Sea salt and pepper to taste
- ½ cup cornstarch
- ¼ cup olive oil
- 2 large eggs, beaten

For Sauce:

- ½ cup apple cider vinegar
- ½ cup brown sugar
- ¼ cup ketchup

- ¼ cup soy sauce
- ¼ cup water
- 1 teaspoon garlic, minced

Directions:

1. In a mixing bowl whisk together, the sauce ingredients. In a separate bowl, season the chicken with salt and pepper, then stir in cornstarch and eggs.
2. Heat olive oil in large pan over medium-high heat. Cook chicken until a light golden brown for about 5 minutes on each side.
3. Transfer chicken to Crock Pot and cover it in sweet and sour sauce. Stir to evenly coat chicken, then cover and cook on HIGH for 3 hours. Serve over brown rice or noodles.

Nutrition:

Calories: 387

Fat: 16 g

Carbs: 19 g Proteins: 35 g

CHAPTER 3:

Sides

10. Cauliflower and Almonds

Preparation time: 10 minutes

Cooking time: 3 hours

Servings: 2

Ingredients:

- 2 cups cauliflower florets
- 2 oz. tomato paste
- 1 small yellow onion, chopped
- 1 tablespoon chives, chopped
- Salt and black pepper to the taste

- 1 tablespoon almonds, sliced

Directions:

1. In your crock pot, mix the cauliflower with the tomato paste and the other ingredients, toss, cook on high within 3 hours. Divide between plates and serve as a side dish.

Nutrition:

Calories: 177

Fat: 12g

Carbs: 20g

Protein: 7g

11. Rosemary Leeks

Preparation time: 10 minutes

Cooking time: 3 hours

Servings: 2

Ingredients:

- ½ tablespoon olive oil
- ½ leeks, sliced ½ cup tomato sauce
- 2 garlic cloves, minced
- Salt and black pepper to the taste
- ¼ tablespoon rosemary, chopped

Directions:

1. In your crock pot, mix the leeks with the oil, sauce, and the other ingredients, toss, put the lid on, cook on high for 3 hours, divide between plates and serve as a side dish.

Nutrition: Calories: 202 Fat: 2g Carbs: 18g Protein: 8g

12. Broccoli Rabe

Preparation Time: 15 minutes Cooking time: 1 hour

Servings: 3 Ingredients:

- 4 oz bacon, chopped, cooked
- 10 oz broccoli rabe, chopped
- 2 oz Parmesan, grated
- 1 teaspoon salt
- 1 teaspoon chili flakes
- 1 teaspoon ground black pepper
- ¼ cup almond milk, unsweetened
- 1 teaspoon butter

Directions:

1. Mix the chopped broccoli rabe and cooked bacon. Transfer the mixture to the crockpot. Add the grated Parmesan, salt, chili flakes, ground black pepper and almond milk.

2. Stir gently and add butter. Close the lid and cook the meal for 1 hour on High. Transfer the hot cooked meal onto serving plates and enjoy!

Nutrition:

Calories 347

Fat 25.9g

Carbs 6.2g

Protein 22.9g

13. Soft Keto Kale Salad

Preparation Time: 15 minutes

Cooking time: 30 minutes

Servings: 4

Ingredients:

- 6 oz bacon, chopped, cooked
- 1 oz almond, chopped
- 1 tablespoon olive oil
- 1 cup Italian dark-leaf kale, chopped
- ¾ cup almond milk, unsweetened
- 1 cucumber, chopped
- 1 garlic clove, diced

Directions:

1. Place the chopped kale, almond milk, and diced garlic in the crockpot. Close the lid and cook the kale for 30 minutes on High.

2. Meanwhile, place the chopped cucumbers in the salad bowl. Add olive oil, bacon, and chopped almond.

3. When the kale is cooked, transfer it immediately to the salad bowl and stir. Serve it warm!

Nutrition:

Calories 423

Fat 35.6g

Carbs 8.4g

Protein 19.3g

14. Keto Leeks

Preparation Time: 10 minutes

Cooking time: 2 hours

Servings: 3

Ingredients:

- 8 oz leek, sliced 1 tablespoon butter
- 1 tablespoon full-fat cream cheese
- 1 teaspoon ground black pepper
- ¼ teaspoon minced garlic

Directions:

1. Place the sliced leek, butter, cream cheese, ground black pepper, and minced garlic in the crockpot. Stir the ingredients and close the lid. Cook the leeks for 2 hours on High. Stir the cooked leeks and serve!

Nutrition: Calories 52 Fat 2.5g Carbs 6.9g Protein 1.2g

CHAPTER 4:

Seafood

15. Shrimp and Rice Mix

Preparation Time: 5 minutes

Cooking Time: 1 hour and 30 minutes

Servings: 2

Ingredients:

- 1 pound shrimp, peeled and deveined
- 1 cup chicken stock
- ½ cup wild rice
- ½ cup carrots, peeled and cubed
- 1 green bell pepper, cubed

- ½ teaspoon turmeric powder
- ½ teaspoon coriander, ground
- 1 tablespoon olive oil
- 1 red onion, chopped
- A pinch of salt and black pepper
- 1 tablespoon cilantro, chopped

Directions:

1. In your crockpot, mix the stock with the rice, carrots and the other ingredients except the shrimp, toss, put the lid on and cook on High for 1 hour.
2. Add the shrimp, toss, put the lid back on and cook on High for 30 minutes. Divide the mix between plates and serve.

Nutrition:

Calories 232

Fat 9

Carbs 6 Protein 8

16. Shrimp and Red Chard

Preparation Time: 5 minutes

Cooking Time: 1 hour

Servings: 2

Ingredients:

- 1-pound shrimp, peeled and deveined
- Juice of 1 lime
- 1 cup red chard, torn
- ½ cup tomato sauce
- 2 garlic cloves, minced
- 1 red onion, sliced
- 1 tablespoon olive oil
- ½ teaspoon sweet paprika
- A pinch of salt and black pepper
- 1 tablespoon parsley, chopped

Directions:

1. In your crockpot, mix the shrimp with the lime juice, chard and the other ingredients, toss, put the lid on and cook on High for 1 hour. Divide the mix into bowls and serve.

Nutrition:

Calories 200

Fat 13g

Carbs 6g

Protein 11g

17. Chives Mussels

Preparation Time: 5 minutes

Cooking Time: 1 hour

Servings: 2

Ingredients:

- 1-pound mussels, debearded
- ½ teaspoon coriander, ground
- ½ teaspoon rosemary, dried
- 1 tablespoon lime zest, grated
- Juice of 1 lime
- 1 cup tomato passata
- ¼ cup chicken stock
- A pinch of salt and black pepper
- 1 tablespoon chives, chopped

Directions:

1. In your crockpot, mix the mussels with the coriander, rosemary and the other ingredients, toss, put the lid on and cook on High for 1 hour. Divide the mix into bowls and serve.

Nutrition:

Calories 200

Fat 12g

Carbs 6g

Protein 9g

18. Calamari and Sauce

Preparation Time: 10 minutes

Cooking Time: 2 hours

Servings: 2

Ingredients:

- 1-pound calamari rings
- 2 scallions, chopped
- 2 garlic cloves, minced
- ½ cup heavy cream
- ½ cup chicken stock
- 1 tablespoon lime juice
- ½ cup black olives, pitted and halved
- A pinch of salt and black pepper
- 2 tablespoons chives, chopped

Directions:

1. In your crockpot, mix the calamari with the scallions, garlic and the other ingredients except the cream, toss, put the lid on and cook on High for 1 hour.
2. Add the cream, toss, cook on High for 1 more hour, divide into bowls and serve.

Nutrition:

Calories 200

Fat 12g

Carbs 5g

Protein 6g

19. Salmon Salad

Preparation Time: 5 minutes

Cooking Time: 3 hours

Servings: 2

Ingredients:

- 1-pound salmon fillets, boneless and cubed
- ¼ cup chicken stock
- 1 zucchini, cut with a spiralizer
- 1 carrot, sliced
- 1 eggplant, cubed
- ½ cup cherry tomatoes, halved
- 1 red onion, sliced
- ½ teaspoon turmeric powder
- ½ teaspoon chili powder
- ½ tablespoon rosemary, chopped

- A pinch of salt and black pepper
- 1 tablespoon chives, chopped

Directions:

1. In your crockpot, mix the salmon with the zucchini, stock, carrot and the other ingredients, toss, put the lid on and cook on High for 3 hours. Divide the mix into bowls and serve.

Nutrition:

Calories 424

Fat 15.1g

Carbs 28.1g

Protein 49g

CHAPTER 5:

Poultry

20. Filipino Chicken Adobo

Preparation time: 15 minutes

Cooking time: 3 hours & 30 minutes

Servings: 6

Ingredients:

- ¾ cup plain rice vinegar
- ½ cup low-sodium soy sauce
- 4 cloves garlic, pressed
- 1 (2- to 3-inch) piece fresh ginger, peeled and grated (optional)
- 1 tablespoon light brown sugar

- 1 teaspoon black peppercorns
- 2 bay leaves
- 2½ pounds (1.1 kg) bone-in, skin-on chicken thighs (about 8), trimmed of fat
- 1 pound (454 g) red or Yukon gold potatoes, scrubbed and cut into eights
- 2 medium-size carrots, sliced, or 2 cups baby carrots
- 4 ounces (113 g) green beans, ends trimmed
- 2 tablespoons olive oil
- ¾ cup water

Directions:

1. In a shallow glass baking dish, stir together the vinegar, soy sauce, garlic, ginger (if using), brown sugar, peppercorns, and bay leaves.
2. Add the chicken and turn to coat. Cover and marinate in the refrigerator for at least 1 hour or as long as overnight.

3. Place the potatoes, carrots, and green beans in the crock pot. Lift the chicken out of the marinade and pat dry with paper towels.

4. Heat the oil in a large skillet over medium-high heat and cook the chicken, skin side down, until it is a golden brown on both sides, about 2 minutes per side.

5. Transfer the chicken thighs to the crock. Pour the marinade and water into the skillet and bring to a boil. Pour the sauce into the crock.

6. Cover and cook on high for 3 to 3½ hours, or until the juice of the chicken runs clear. Discard the bay leaves. Serve the chicken and vegetables with the sauce.

Nutrition:

Calories: 362

Carbs: 7g

Fat: 22g

Protein: 33g

21. Tarragon Chicken Marsala

Preparation time: 15 minutes

Cooking time: 3-4 hours

Servings: 6

Ingredients:

- ¾ cup all-purpose flour or rice flour, for dredging
- 6 boneless, skin-on chicken breast halves (about 2 pounds / 907 g)
- 3 tablespoons unsalted butter or ghee
- 2 medium-size shallots, minced
- 8 ounces (227 g) sliced white or cremini mushrooms
- 1 (14½-ounce / 411-g) can low-sodium chicken broth
- Sea salt and freshly ground black pepper, to taste
- Marsala Gravy:
- 2 (1.2-ounce / 34-g) packages chicken gravy mix, such as Knorr

- 1/3 cup dry Marsala wine
- 2 teaspoons finely chopped fresh tarragon

Directions:

1. Put the flour in a shallow dish or pie plate. One piece at a time, dredge the chicken in the flour, coating both sides and shaking off any excess flour.
2. Heat the butter in a large skillet over medium-high heat. When the butter is foaming, add the chicken, skin side down. Cook the chicken until it is a deep golden brown on both sides, about 5 minutes per side.
3. Transfer the chicken pieces to the crock pot. Add the shallots and mushrooms to the skillet and cook over high heat, stirring, until they are slightly brown.
4. Transfer to the crock. Add the broth to the skillet and bring to a boil, stirring, to dissolve any brown particles that are stuck to the pan.

5. Pour the broth over the chicken in the crock. Season with salt and pepper. Cover and cook on high for 3 to 4 hours, until the chicken pulls apart easily.

6. Ladle 2 cups of the liquid out of the crock pot and into a saucepan. Discard any remaining liquid. Add the two gravy packets, Marsala, and tarragon to the saucepan and whisk well.

7. Cook over medium-high heat, whisking constantly, and bring to a boil. Reduce the heat to a simmer and cook for 2 minutes, until thickened and smooth.

8. While the gravy simmers, remove the chicken breasts and mushrooms from the crock, discard the skin, and shred or chop the meat into large pieces. Serve the gravy over the warm chicken and mushrooms.

Nutrition:

Calories: 357

Carbs: 8g

Fat: 7g Protein: 56g

22. Garlicky Lemon-Thyme Turkey Legs

Preparation time: 15 minutesCooking time: 6-8 hours

Servings: 6

Ingredients:

- 8 cloves garlic, peeled
- Grated zest of 4 lemons
- 2 teaspoons fresh thyme leaves
- Salt and freshly ground black pepper, to taste
- ¼ cup extra-virgin olive oil
- 6 turkey legs, skin removed
- ½ cup dry white wine
- 1 cup chicken broth

Directions:

1. Put the garlic, zest, thyme, 1½ teaspoons salt, ½ teaspoon pepper, and oil in a food processor or blender and blend to a

paste. Rub the paste on the turkey and put the turkey in the crock pot.

2. Pour the wine and chicken broth in the insert of a crock pot. Cover and cook on low for 6 to 8 hours, until the turkey is cooked through and registers 175°F (79°C) on an instant-read thermometer.
3. Remove the legs from the sauce and cover with aluminum foil. Strain the sauce through a fine-mesh sieve into a saucepan and bring to a boil. Season with salt and pepper before serving.

Nutrition:

Calories: 413

Carbs: 3g

Fat: 31g

Protein: 31g

23. Turkey Teriyaki Thighs

Preparation time: 15 minutes

Cooking time: 3-4 hours

Servings: 6

Ingredients:

- ½ cup soy sauce
- 2 tablespoons hoisin sauce
- 2 cloves garlic, minced
- 1 teaspoon freshly grated ginger
- 2 tablespoons rice wine (mirin) or dry sherry
- ¼ firmly packed light brown sugar
- 4 turkey thighs, skin removed

Directions:

1. Blend the soy sauce, hoisin, garlic, ginger, rice wine, and brown sugar in a mixing bowl and stir to combine.

2. Pour the marinade in a zipper-top plastic bag. Add the turkey thighs to the bag. Seal the bag and refrigerate for at least 8 hours or overnight. Pour the contents of the bag in the insert of a crock pot.

3. Cover and cook on high for 3 to 4 hours, until the turkey is cooked through and registers 175°F (79°C) on an instant-read thermometer.

4. Remove the turkey from the crock pot, cover with aluminum foil, and allow to rest for 20 minutes before serving.

Nutrition:

Calories: 201

Carbs: 8g

Fat: 6g

Protein: 29g

24. Chicken Pate

Preparation time: 15 minutes Cooking Time: 8 Hours

Servings:6 Ingredients:

- 1 carrot, peeled
- 1 teaspoon salt
- 1-pound chicken liver
- 2 cups of water
- 2 tablespoons coconut oil

Directions:

1. Chop the carrot roughly and put it in the Crock Pot. Add chicken liver and water. Cook the mixture for 8 hours on Low.
2. Then drain water and transfer the mixture in the blender. Add coconut oil and salt. Blend the mixture until smooth. Store the pate in the fridge for up to 7 days.

Nutrition: Calories 169 Protein 18.6g Carbohydrates 1.7g Fat 9.5g

CHAPTER 6:

Meat

25. Pork Tenderloin

Preparation time: 10 minutes

Cooking time: 4 hours

Servings: 6

Ingredients

- 1 ½ lbs. pork tenderloin, trimmed and cut in half lengthwise
- garlic cloves, chopped
- 1 oz envelope dry onion soup mix
- ¾ cup red wine
- 1 cup water

- Pepper and salt

Directions:

1. Place pork tenderloin into the crockpot. Pour red wine and water over pork. Sprinkle dry onion soup mix on top of pork tenderloin.

2. Top with chopped garlic and season with pepper and salt. Cover crockpot with lid and cook on low for 4 hours. Stir well and serve.

Nutrition:

Calories 196

Fat 4 g

Carbohydrates 3.1 g

Protein 29.9 g

26. Smoky Pork with Cabbage

Preparation time: 10 minutes

Cooking time: 8 hours

Servings: 6

Ingredients

- 1 lbs. pastured pork roast
- 1/3 cup liquid smoke
- 1/2 cabbage head, chopped
- 1 cup water
- 1 tbsp. kosher salt

Directions:

1. Rub pork with kosher salt and place into the crockpot. Pour liquid smoke over the pork. Add water. Cover crockpot with lid and cook on low for 7 hours.
2. Remove pork from the crockpot and add cabbage to the bottom of the crockpot. Now place pork on top of the cabbage.

3. Cover again and cook for 1 hour more. Shred pork with a fork and serves.

Nutrition:

Calories 484

Fat 21.5 g

Carbohydrates 3.5 g

Protein 65.4 g

27. Roasted Pork Shoulder

Preparation time: 10 minutes Cooking time: 9 hours

Servings: 8 Ingredients

- 1 lbs. pork shoulder
- 1 tsp garlic powder
- 1/2 cup water
- 1/2 tsp black pepper
- 1/2 tsp sea salt

Directions:

1. Season pork with garlic powder, pepper, and salt and place in a crockpot. Add water. Cover crockpot with lid and cook on high for 1 hour, then turn heat to low and cook for 8 hours.
2. Remove meat from the crockpot and shred using a fork. Serve and enjoy.

Nutrition: Calories 664 Fat 48.5 g Carbohydrates 0.3 g Protein 52.9 g

28. Chili Lime Beef

Preparation time: 10 minutes

Cooking time: 6 hours

Servings: 4

Ingredients

- 1 lb. beef chuck roast
- 1 tsp chili powder
- 2 cups lemon-lime soda
- 1 fresh lime juice
- 1 garlic clove, crushed
- 1/2 tsp salt

Directions:

1. Place beef chuck roast into the crockpot. Season roast with garlic, chili powder, and salt. Pour lemon-lime soda over the roast.

2. Cover crockpot with lid and cook on low for 6 hours. Shred the meat using a fork. Add lime juice over shredded roast and serve.

Nutrition:

Calories 355

Fat 16.8 g

Carbohydrates 14 g

Protein 35.5 g

29. Beef in Sauce

Preparation time: 10 minutes

Cooking time: 9 hours

Servings: 4

Ingredients

- 1-pound beef stew meat, chopped
- 1 teaspoon gram masala
- 1 cup of water
- 1 tablespoon flour
- 1 teaspoon garlic powder
- 1 onion, diced

Directions

1. Whisk flour with water until smooth and pour the liquid into the crockpot. Add gram masala and beef stew meat.

2. After this, add onion and garlic powder. Close the lid and cook the meat on low for 9 hours. Serve the cooked beef with thick gravy from the crockpot.

Nutrition:

Calories 231

Protein 35g

Carbohydrates 4.6g

Fat 7.1g

CHAPTER 7:

Vegetables

30. Asparagus with Lemon

Preparation time: 10 minutes

Cooking Time: 2 hours

Servings: 2

Ingredients:

- 1 lb. asparagus spears
- 1 tbsp lemon juice

Directions:

1. Prepare the seasonings: 2 crushed cloves of garlic and salt and pepper to taste. Put the asparagus spears on the bottom of the

crockpot. Add the lemon juice and the seasonings. Cook on low for 2 hours.

Nutrition:

Calories: 78

Fat: 2 g

Carbs: 3.7 g

Protein: 9 g

31. Veggie-Noodle Soup

Preparation time: 10 minutes

Cooking Time: 8 hours

Servings: 2

Ingredients:

- 1/2 cup chopped carrots, chopped
- 1/2 cup chopped celery, chopped
- 1 tsp Italian seasoning
- 7 oz zucchini, cut spiral
- 2 cups spinach leaves, chopped

Directions:

1. Except for the zucchini and spinach, add all the ingredients to the crockpot. Add 3 cups of water. Add 1/2 cup of chopped onion and garlic, 1/8 tsp of salt and pepper and desired spices such as thyme and bay leaves if desired.

2. Cover and cook for 8 hours on low. Add the zucchini and spinach at the last 10 minutes of cooking.

Nutrition:

Calories: 56

Fat: 0.5 g

Carbs: 0.5 g

Protein: 3 g

32. Zucchini and Yellow Squash

Preparation time: 10 minutes

Cooking Time: 6 hours

Servings: 2

Ingredients:

- 2/3 cup zucchini, sliced
- 2/3 cups yellow squash, sliced
- 1/3 tsp Italian seasoning
- 1/8 cup butter

Directions:

1. Place zucchini and squash on the bottom of the crockpot. Sprinkle with the Italian seasoning with salt, pepper and garlic powder to taste. Top with butter. Cover and cook for 6 hours on low.

Nutrition: Calories: 122 Fat: 9.9 g Carbs: 3.7 g Protein: 4.2 g

33. Cauliflower Bolognese on Zucchini Noodles

Preparation time: 10 minutes

Cooking Time: 4 hours

Servings: 2

Ingredients:

- 1 cauliflower head, floret cuts
- 1 tsp dried basil flakes
- 28 oz diced tomatoes
- 1/2 cup vegetable broth
- 5 zucchinis, spiral cut

Directions:

1. Place ingredients in the crockpot except for the zucchini. Season with 2 garlic cloves, 3.4 diced onions, salt and pepper to taste and desired spices.

2. Cover and cook for 4 hours. Smash florets of the cauliflower with a fork to form "bolognese." Transfer the dish on top of the zucchini noodles.

Nutrition:

Calories: 164

Fat: 5 g

Carbs: 6 g

Protein: 12 g

34. Shredded Cabbage Sauté

Preparation time: 15 minutes Cooking time: 6 hours

Servings: 4 Ingredients:

- 2 cups white cabbage, shredded
- 1 cup tomato juice
- 1 teaspoon salt
- 1 teaspoon sugar
- 1 teaspoon dried oregano
- 1 tablespoons olive oil
- 1 cup of water

Directions:

1. Put all ingredients in the crockpot. Carefully mix all ingredients with the help of the spoon and close the lid. Cook the cabbage sauté for 6 hours on Low.

Nutrition: Calories 118 Protein 1.2 g Carbs 6.9 g Fat 10.6 g

35. Ranch Broccoli

Preparation time: 15 minutes

Cooking time: 1 hour & 30 minutes

Servings: 3

Ingredients:

- 2 cups broccoli
- 1 teaspoon chili flakes
- 2 tablespoons ranch dressing
- 2 cups of water

Directions:

1. Put the broccoli in the crockpot. Add water and close the lid. Cook the broccoli on high for 1.5 hours.
2. Then drain water and transfer the broccoli in the bowl. Sprinkle it with chili flakes and ranch dressing. Shake the meal gently.

Nutrition: Calories 34 Protein 2.7 g Carbs 6.6 g Fat 0.3 g

36. Sautéed Spinach

Preparation time: 15 minutes Cooking time: 1 hour

Servings: 3

Ingredients:

- 2 cups spinach
- 1 tablespoon vegan butter, softened
- 2 cups of water
- 1 oz Parmesan, grated
- 1 teaspoon pine nuts, crushed

Directions:

1. Chop the spinach and put it in the crockpot. Add water and close the lid. Cook the spinach on High for 1 hour.
2. Then drain water and put the cooked spinach in the bowl. Add pine nuts, Parmesan, and butter. Carefully mix the spinach.

Nutrition: Calories 108 Protein 7.1 g Carbs 1.9 g Fat 8.7 g

CHAPTER 8:

Soups & Stews

37. Lamb and Eggplant Stew

Preparation Time: 15 minutes

Cooking Time: 8 hours & 30 minutes

Servings: 4

Ingredients:

- 1 ½ lb. Minced lamb
- 1 Onion, finely chopped
- 3 Garlic cloves, crushed
- ½ Large eggplant, cut into small cubes
- 1 Tomatoes, chopped

- 1 Lamb stock cube
- 1 tsp Dried rosemary
- ¾ cup Grated mozzarella
- 2 tbsp Olive oil
- 2 cups Water
- Salt and pepper to taste

Directions:

1. Add olive oil into the Crock-Pot. Add water, lamb, onion, garlic, eggplant, stock cube, tomatoes, rosemary, salt, and pepper to the pot. Stir to mix.
2. Cook within 8 hours, high. Remove the lid and stir the stew. Sprinkle the mozzarella on top, cover with the lid, and cook 30 minutes more. Serve.

Nutrition:

Calories: 432

Fat: 21g Carbs: 8.8g Protein: 50.9g

38. Bacon and Cauliflower Soup

Preparation Time: 15 minutes

Cooking Time: 4 hours

Servings: 4

Ingredients:

- ¾ Large cauliflower head, cut into chunks
- 3 Garlic cloves, crushed
- ¾ Onion, finely chopped
- 4 Bacon slices, cut into small pieces
- 2 cups Chicken stock
- ½ tsp Smoked paprika
- ½ tsp Chili powder
- ¾ cup Heavy cream
- 2 tbsp Olive oil
- Salt and pepper to taste

- Paprika to taste

Directions:

1. Add olive oil into the Crock-Pot. Add the garlic, cauliflower, onion, bacon, stock, paprika, chili, salt, and pepper to the pot. Stir to mix.
2. Cook on high within 4 hours. Open the lid and blend with a hand mixer. Add the cream and mix. Serve sprinkled with paprika.

Nutrition:

Calories: 265

Fat: 22.3g

Carbs: 6.1g

Protein: 10.4g

39. Southern Paleo Crock Pot Chili

Preparation Time: 10 minutes

Cooking Time: 8 hours

Servings: 6

Ingredients:

- 1/2 tsp sea salt
- 1 tsp paprika
- 1 diced big onion
- 1 tsp onion powder 1 tsp garlic powder
- 1 tbsp. Worcestershire sauce
- 1 lb. grass-fed organic beef
- 1 tbsp. fresh parsley, chopped
- 1 seeded & diced green bell pepper
- 4 tsp chili powder
- 4 chopped small big large carrots

- 26 oz. tomatoes, neatly chopped
- a pinch of cumin diced onions, if desired
- sliced Jalapeños, if desired
- dairy-free sour cream, if desired

Directions:

1. Using a medium-sized skillet, add in the ground beef and brown over high heat, occasionally stirring until there is no pink. Put the browned beef inside the crockpot, including the fat.
2. Add in the onion, green bell pepper, tomatoes, and carrots into the crockpot. Mix all the fixing, then put in all the remaining seasonings and spices.
3. Stir all the ingredients together again, then cover and cook for 8 hours on low settings or 5 on high settings. Serve then top with sour cream (dairy-free) with extra jalapenos, if desired, and enjoy.

Nutrition: Calories: 241 Carbs: 24g Fat: 8g Protein: 20g

40. Dairy-Free Chili Chicken Soup

Preparation Time: 30 minutes

Cooking Time: 6 hours

Servings: 10

Ingredients:

- 1/4 teaspoon white pepper
- 1 cup of coconut milk
- 1 teaspoon chili powder
- 1 big diced yellow onion
- 1 tablespoon minced garlic
- 1 tablespoon coarse-real salt
- 2 teaspoons cumin
- 2 cups chicken broth
- 2 (8 ounces) cans green chilies, diced
- 2 & ½-pounds boneless chicken thighs

- 3 cans Great Northern beans
- Optional:
- 1/4 cup arrowroot starch
- 1/2 cup water

For toppings:

- 1/3 cup chopped cilantro
- sour cream
- tortilla chips
- juiced lime

Directions:

1. Put all the items into the crockpot, then cover and cook for 5-6 hours on high settings. Remove the chicken from the crockpot, then transfer into a medium-sized bowl, then shred.
2. Take the chicken back inside the crockpot, then stir until properly distributed, then allow to cook for an extra 30 minutes.

3. Taste for seasoning as desired. Serve then garnish with any toppings of your choice and enjoy.

Nutrition:

Calories: 137

Carbs: 9g

Fat: 2g

Protein: 0g

41. Cheeseburger Soup

Preparation Time: 15 minutes

Cooking Time: 3 hours

Servings: 5

Ingredients:

- 1/2 tsp salt
- 1/2 tsp pepper
- 1/2 cup cheese
- 1/2 cup chopped onions
- 1/2 chopped red bell pepper
- 1 tsp garlic powder
- 1 tsp Worcestershire sauce
- 1 1/2 tsp parsley
- 1 1/2 chopped tomatoes
- 1 1/2 pounds ground beef

- 2 chopped & cooked bacon slices
- 3 cups beef broth
- 3 chopped celery sticks
- 8 ounces tomato paste

Directions:

1. Using a large saucepan, add in the ground beef and brown. Halfway through the browning process, drain off every fat, add in the red pepper, onions, celery, and continue cooking.
2. Add the remaining ingredients and beef mixture into the crockpot then stir to combine.
3. If desired, add in more beef broth, cover, and cook for 6-8 hours on low setting or 3-5 hours on a high setting, occasionally stirring.
4. Serve then top with a full spoon of cheese and bacon slices (if desired), then enjoy.

Nutrition:

Calories: 200 Carbs: 14g Fat: 13g Protein: 7g

CHAPTER 9:

Snacks

42. 2-Ingredient Cheese Dip

Preparation Time: 10 minutes Cooking Time: 2 hours

Servings: 20 Ingredients:

- 16 ounces Velveeta cheese, cubed 1 (16-ounce) jar salsa

Directions:

1. In a large crockpot, place cheese and salsa and stir gently to combine. Set the crockpot on High and cook, covered, for about 2 hours, stirring occasionally. Serve hot.

Nutrition:

Calories: 71

Carbohydrates: 3.9g Protein: 4.4g Fat: 4.9g

43. Stunning Pizza Dip

Preparation Time: 10 minutes

Cooking Time: 2 hours

Servings: 32

Ingredients:

- 1 (16-ounce) jar sugar-free pizza sauce
- 1 cup cooked grass-fed chicken, chopped
- 4 ounces olives, chopped
- ½ cup yellow onion, chopped
- 1 (8-ounce) package cream cheese, softened
- 8 ounces mozzarella cheese, shredded

Directions:

1. In a bowl, add all ingredients except cream cheese and mozzarella and mix well. In the bottom of a greased crockpot, spread cream cheese evenly and top with onion mixture evenly.

2. Sprinkle evenly with the mozzarella cheese. Set the crockpot on Low and cook, covered, for about 2 hours. Serve hot.

Nutrition:

Calories: 64

Carbohydrates: 2.5g

Protein: 4.1g

Fat: 4.3g

44. Classic Hamburger Dip

Preparation Time: 15 minutes

Cooking Time: 2 hours 5 minutes

Servings: 20

Ingredients:

- 2 pounds ground lean grass-fed beef
- 1 cup yellow onion, chopped
- 2 garlic cloves, minced
- 1 (4-ounce) can mild chili peppers, chopped
- 2 (6-ounce) cans sugar-free tomato sauce
- 16 ounces cream cheese, cubed
- ½ cup Parmesan cheese, grated
- ½ cup sugar-free ketchup
- 1 teaspoon dried oregano
- 1½ teaspoons red chili powder

- ½ teaspoon ground cumin
- Salt and freshly ground black pepper, to taste

Directions:

1. Heat a heavy skillet over medium heat and cook ground beef and onion for about 4-5 minutes. Drain grease from meat mixture.
2. Transfer beef mixture into a crockpot with remaining ingredients and stir to combine. Set the crockpot on Low and cook, covered, for about 2 hours. Serve hot.

Nutrition:

Calories:195

Carbohydrates: 4.3g

Protein: 17.5g

Fat: 12g

45. Zippy Broccoli Dip

Preparation Time: 20 minutes

Cooking Time: 2¼ hours

Servings: 12

Ingredients:

- 6 center cut bacon slices, chopped
- ½ large yellow onion, chopped
- 2 garlic cloves, minced
- ¼ teaspoon red pepper flakes
- 4 cups fresh broccoli florets, chopped
- 8 ounces cream cheese, softened
- 1 cup Colby-Jack cheese, shredded
- ½ cup Parmesan cheese, grated
- 1 tablespoon scallions, copped
- ½ cup sour cream

- ½ cup unsweetened almond milk
- ½ cup mayonnaise
- 1½ teaspoons Worcestershire sauce
- Salt and freshly ground black pepper, to taste

Directions:

1. Heat a large sauté pan over medium heat and cook bacon for about 8-10 minutes. With a slotted spoon, transfer the bacon onto a paper towel-lined plate to drain.
2. Drain bacon grease from pan, leaving about 2 teaspoons. In the same pan, add onion with a pinch of salt and black pepper and cook for about 3-4 minutes.
3. Add garlic and red pepper flakes and cook for about 1 minute. Transfer the onion mixture and bacon into a greased crockpot with remaining ingredients and stir to combine.
4. Set the crockpot on Low and cook, covered, for about 2 hours.

Nutrition:Calories: 427 Carbohydrates: 10.6g Protein: 19.2g Fat: 34.6g

46. Cheese Sticks

Preparation time: 15 minutes Cooking Time: 2.5 Hours

Servings: 8 Ingredients:

- 4 eggs, beaten
- 1 cup Cheddar cheese, shredded
- 1 tablespoon fresh dill, chopped
- 1 tablespoon chives, chopped
- 1 teaspoon turmeric powder
- 1 teaspoon butter, softened
- 1/3 cup almond flour
- 1 teaspoon salt

Directions:

1. In the mixing bowl, mix up together beaten eggs, cheese and the other ingredients. You should get a soft homogenous mixture. Line the bottom of the crockpot with the baking paper.

2. Transfer the cheese mixture in the crockpot and flatten well. Close the lid and bake it for 2.5 hours on High. Then chill the cooked mixture very well and cut into the serving sticks.

Nutrition:

Calories 304

Fat 8.3g

Carbs 1.6g

Protein 7g

CHAPTER 10:

Desserts

47. Lemon Cake

Preparation time: 15 minutes Cooking time: 3 hours

Servings: 5

Ingredients:

For the cake:

- 1 ½ cup almond flour
- ½ cup coconut flour
- 3 tsp Puree all-purpose (or Swerve)
- 2 tsp baking powder
- ½ tsp xanthan gum optional

- ½ cup butter melted
- ½ cup whipping cream
- 2 tbsp Juice of lemon
- 2 Zest from lemon
- 2 Eggs

Topping:

- 3 tsp Puree all-purpose (or Swerve)
- 2 tsp baking powder
- ½ cup boiling water
- 2 tbsp butter melted
- 2 tbsp lemon juice

Directions:

1. For the cake, put the coconut flour, sweetener, almond flour, baking powder, xanthan gum in a medium-sized bowl. Stir well everything

2. In another bowl whisk the butter, squeeze the lemon juice, xanthan gum, whipping cream, zest, crack the egg in a bowl. Combine both mixtures dry and wet one.

3. Spray the cooking spray over the Crock Pot, pour the mixture into the Crock Pot. Cover and put on high for 3 hours until the inserted in the center knife comes out clean.

4. While the cake is cooking, prepare the topping – conjoin the baking powder, water, melted butter and lemon juice.

5. Take off the cake once it is ready for a large plate. Pour the topping over it. Add whipped cream or fresh fruits by serving, if desired. Bon Appetite!

Nutrition:

Calories: 490

Carbs: 67g

Fat: 23g

Protein: 5g

48. Raspberry-Vanilla Pudding Cake

Preparation time: 15 minutes Cooking time: 0 hours

Servings: 10 Ingredients:

- 2 cups Sweetener
- 2 cups almond flour
- 4 tsp baking powder
- 1 tsp salt
- 1 cup milk
- 4 tbsp butter
- 1 tsp vanilla
- 2 container fresh raspberries (6 oz)
- 1 tbsp vanilla pudding mix
- 1 ¾ cup boiling water
- some fresh raspberries for dressing

  .
- Vanilla or whipped cream

Directions:

1. Take a medium bowl, combine flour, sweetener, baking powder, vanilla, salt, milk. Whisk everything. Melt the butter and add to the mixture.

2. Open the container with raspberries and pour them into the mixture. Spread the cooking spray over the sides and bottom of the Crock Pot.

3. Put the mixture into the Crock Pot and spread it on the bottom. Sprinkle the pudding mix over the top of the mixture but don't stir it.

4. Take a little bowl, let the water boil. Pour the water carefully over the top of the pudding mix and the mixture.

5. Cover and put on high for 2 hours. The ready-made pudding will be on the bottom of the cake. Serve with whipping cream or vanilla and fresh raspberries.

Nutrition: Calories: 322 Carbs: 63g Fat: 7g Protein: 3g

49. Mocha Pudding Cake

Preparation time: 15 minutes

Cooking time: 3 hours

Servings: 10

Ingredients:

- ¾ cup Butter
- 2 oz unsweetened chocolate
- ½ cup heavy cream
- 2 tbsp instant coffee crystals
- 1 tsp vanilla extract
- 4 tbsp cocoa powder
- 1/3 cup almond flour
- 1/8 tsp salt
- 5 eggs, large
- 2/3 cup Stevia

- coconut oil spray for the sides and bottom of the Crock Pot
- Optional: whipped cream for serving

Directions:

1. Cut butter into large chunks. Chop finely unsweetened chocolate. Spray the bottom of the Crock Pot with cooking spray.
2. Take a little bowl, melt butter together with unsweetened chocolate. Whisk it all the time, don't let it burn. Set aside and let it cool.
3. Take another medium bowl, whisk coffee crystals, heavy cream, vanilla extract. Take one more bowl and combine the cocoa, salt, almond flour. Stir well.
4. Using a mixer or a blender, whisk the eggs on a high speed until thickened slightly. Add sweetener. Turn the speed of the mixer (or blender) on low, pour the butter with chocolate. Continue mixing.
5. Stir almond flour, salt and cocoa mixture too. Add also to the blending mixture coffee, cream and vanilla mix.

6. Pour the compound into the Crock Pot. Put a paper (towel) over the Crock Pot and cover with cap. Put on low for 3 hours.
7. Check the readiness of the cake – the edges must be like a cake, the center – must have a soft consistency. Serve the cake with whipped cream if desired.

Nutrition:

Calories: 230

Carbs: 45g

Fat: 5g

Protein: 6g

50. Black Raspberry Cheesecake

Preparation time: 15 minutes Cooking time: 2 hours

Servings: 8 Ingredients:

- 1 pint black raspberries (fresh)
- 2 tbsp lemon juice
- 16 oz cream cheese softened
- 6 oz Greek-style yogurt
- 2 tsp vanilla extract
- 25 drops liquid stevia
- 2 eggs
- ½ cup black raspberries, for garnish

Directions:

1. Take a medium-sized skillet and put over medium heat, place the raspberries. Stir them frequently. They must reduce the jam. It takes about 15 minutes.

2. Use a potato masher, break the raspberries up. Any pieces must remain. Add lemon juice and let the mixture cool.

3. Take a large bowl combine liquid stevia and cream cheese, Greek yogurt, vanilla. Using a blender mix everything well, until the ingredients are blended thoroughly.

4. Add the cracked eggs, one after one blending all the time the mixture. Spray the bottom and the sides of the Crock Pot with cooking spray, pour the egg-cheese mixture into the Crock Pot.

5. Cover and put the dish on high for 2 hours. Check the readiness of the cheesecake – the knife must go out from the cake clean.

6. Take off the cake from the Crock Pot and pour the raspberry on top. Dress with fresh raspberries. Place in the refrigerator for 2 hours. Bon Appetite!

Nutrition:

Calories: 260

Carbs: 20g

Fat: 18g Protein: 4g

Conclusion

You have to the end of this amazing cookbook, but always remember that this is not the end of your cooking journey with the crockpot; but instead, this is your stepping stone towards more cooking glory. We hope you have found your favorite recipes that are time-saving and money-saving.

Now that you know how Crockpot works and the many benefits of using it, maybe it is time for you to buy one for your family, in case you haven't owned one. When it comes to time spent preparing meals for your family, Crock-Pot is a lifesaver. If you are a busy person, a powerful solution is to use the crockpot.

You will also love to own one if you want to make your life simpler at work if you want to make your life simpler at home, and if you want to preserve some of the natural resources. You could also use one if you want to lean towards a healthier lifestyle as cooking in the crockpot is conducive to health than in the oven.

The crockpot can be used in making homemade and custom-made buffets, even in catering services. You can use it for cooking for your staff for special occasions and for showing them how to cook a tasty and healthier dish for your guests well within their own crockpot.

After choosing the best one for you, maybe it is time for you to know more about the recipes you should use. There are various recipes in this cookbook that are perfect for crockpot cooking, and they will definitely be useful and beneficial for you.

Moreover, whether you are a newbie or an experienced cook, you are going to love this cookbook as it is packed with every conceivable taste. You have discovered more than 1000 recipes in this cookbook that you can put into practice using your crockpot. You can always customize the recipes to suit your taste buds, as you can make any recipe mild or hot, sweet or sour; you have all the freedom to make the recipes your own. The best thing about cooking using a crockpot is that you just need to add the main ingredients, and no other complicated cooking preparation is needed; the crockpot will add most of the other ingredients for you.

CPSIA information can be obtained
at www.ICGtesting.com
Printed in the USA
BVHW091955220421
605650BV00002B/167